# HOW TO BE A
# PRINCESS

*Real-Life Fairy Tales for
Modern Heroines*

# HOW TO BE A
# PRINCESS

*Real-Life Fairy Tales for*
*Modern Heroines*

Katy Birchall

*Illustration by Angeline Balayn*

POP PRESS

'Whatever comes,' she said, 'cannot alter one thing. If I am a princess in rags and tatters, I can be a princess inside. It would be easy to be a princess if I were dressed in cloth of gold, but it is a great deal more of a triumph to be one all the time when no one knows it.'

*A Little Princess*
*Frances Hodgson Burnett*

# Contents

Introduction                          8

*Modern princesses ...*

*... are brave*                       11
  Meghan                             13
  Moana                              17
  Ameerah                            21
  Diana, 'Wonder Woman'             25
  Elsa                               29


*... work hard*                       33
  Elizabeth II                       35
  Fiona                              39
  Haya                               43
  Tiana                              47

*. . . are smart* 51

Lalla Salma 53

Leia 57

Kiko 61

Sirindhorn 65

*. . . are kind* 69

Diana 71

Catherine 75

Grace 79

Máxima 83

Rania 87

*. . . are ahead of their time* 91

Margaret 93

Elizabeth I 97

Pingyang 101

Hatshepsut 105

Nzinga 109

Seondeok 113

Acknowledgements 119

Quotation Sources 121

# Introduction
## How do you define a princess?

A pitch-perfect singing voice? Fluent in conversing with woodland creatures? Naturally voluminous locks that always float perfectly behind one shoulder in a sweeping breeze?

Thinking of the princesses today, that won't do. It's just not really ... *enough*.

Sure, Diana, Princess of Wales, had an iconic haircut, but it's not the first thing that comes to mind when we remember her. And what about that other Princess Diana, aka Wonder Woman? She hardly has time to sing while she's leading an army into battle against evil.

What about where she comes from? Does that make a princess? There's got to be some kind of running theme, right?

No, that doesn't pin it down either.

There are, of course, those born into the role, like Queen Elizabeth II and Princess Leia, but then there's also Princess Grace of Monaco, who was a famous Hollywood actress, and Princess Lalla Salma, a computer engineer.

*Fine.*

So, is it what they own?

Nope, that's not it.

Moana set sail with a chicken, not a crown, and you're more likely to see Princess Sirindhorn of Thailand polishing her camera lens than any jewels.

This book tells the stories of the coolest modern princesses around. They are mostly real, sometimes fictional, and all exceptional.

When you're done reading, put this book down and go step into your own regal role. Princesses are made, not born – and I have a feeling you'll make a good one.

Modern princesses

*... are*

*brave*

# Meghan

'With fame comes opportunity, but it also includes responsibility – to advocate and share, to focus less on glass slippers and more on pushing through glass ceilings. And, if I'm lucky enough, to inspire.'

*Meghan Markle*

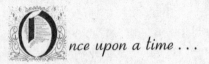

# Once upon a time...

... a young girl named Meghan sat down to write a letter.

She had been watching television in her classroom when a dishwasher soap advertisement flashed up on to the screen. 'Women all over America are fighting greasy pots and pans,' the commercial proclaimed.

Meghan could not get it out of her head.

'In the world of this commercial,' she sighed, 'why is it just *women* in the kitchen, washing pots and pans?' When she got home, she told her father that the wording had bothered her. 'Well,' he smiled, 'you have a voice. Perhaps it is time to use it.'

As Meghan stuck stamps to four different letters, she felt nervous. One of the letters was to the soap manufacturer, one was to civil-rights lawyer Gloria Allred, one to news anchor Linda Ellerbee, and the last one was to then-First Lady, Hillary Clinton. She slid the letters into the postbox and hoped that one of them might hear what she had to say.

All of them heard. They wrote back, inspired by Meghan's conviction in her beliefs. The soap company changed its tagline: '*People* all over America,' the advertisement announced a few weeks later, 'are fighting greasy pots and pans.'

Meghan realised that big change could be sparked even by the smallest of actions. Standing up. Speaking out. Putting pen to paper. And she didn't stop there.

When Meghan grew up to become a talented actress, she understood that along with red carpets, fancy gowns and flashing lights, fame came with the opportunity to make an impact. She spoke up for those who couldn't be heard.

No wonder that when a handsome young prince met her, he felt he had to improve his jokes to get *her* attention. His efforts were not in vain and they happily fell in love.

For from the top of a palace, her voice will be all the louder.

# Moana

'Be the hero or heroine of your

own story, of your own life.'

*Auli'i Cravalho, voice of Disney's Moana*

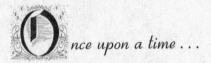 *nce upon a time ...*

... Moana had to make a decision. Spirited, headstrong and drawn to the sea, this chief-in-training had grown up working hard to learn the responsibilities of leadership and earn the respect of her community. Devoted to her family and her people, she knew that she would have to face the dangers of a sea voyage to protect their island and their future. But sometimes, being brave isn't just about facing the challenges ahead. It is also having the courage to leave things behind.

When her island became endangered, Moana had to make a choice.

Leaving her family behind, she set sail across the ocean. She had little experience in sailing or navigation, but she wasn't going to let that stop her. She was going to save her people, no matter how dangerous it was or what the personal cost.

After overcoming all sorts of challenges, once again Moana was faced with a decision. She could give up or she could keep going.

Even though she was scared, Moana found the courage to carry on with her mission. Moana discovered that sometimes you have to be brave enough to step forward when you don't know what lies ahead.

# Ameerah

'Throw yourself to the edge that
you're always scared of. Try
being independent; do it
your way. You'll love it.'

*Princess Ameerah*

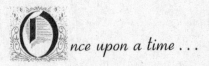

# *O*nce upon a time . . .

. . . Princess Ameerah sat in the driving seat.

In Saudi Arabia, where she lived, women did not have the right to drive and this troubled the princess. Not only did it restrict the freedom of the women in her kingdom, but she also believed it to be symbolic of her nation's other equality issues, such as women's education, their right to work and their participation in politics.

The princess decided it was time for this symbolic driving rule to change. She knew it would not be easy. A lot of powerful people would be very angry at her for attempting to lift this traditional ban.

'We are trying to acquire our own rights, peacefully,' she bravely told them, on behalf of the women in her country. 'We want evolution not a revolution.'

She spoke out loud and clear, relentlessly fighting for this important change, arguing the economic benefits to women driving, as well as the political symbolism. Then she got her international driver's licence so she could drive herself.

From the moment they met, when she interviewed him for her school paper at the age of eighteen, Prince Alwaleed Bin Talal Alsaud admired this young woman's courage, her eloquence and her fierce desire for change.

After an amicable divorce some years later, the prince continued to stand by her side, doing everything in his power to help, such as supporting the first female pilots. 'If a woman can't drive in Saudi Arabia,' he announced stubbornly, 'then she can fly.'

Princess Ameerah knew that it was a long, challenging road ahead to achieve this reform, but she refused to give up.

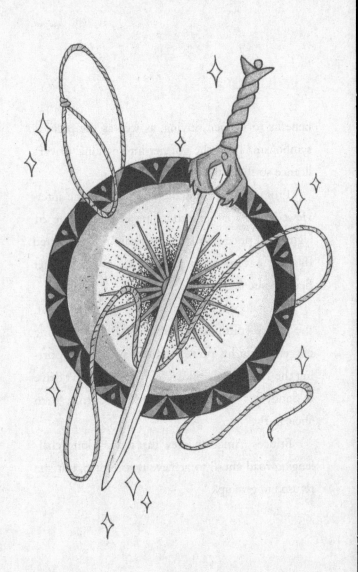

# Diana,
## 'Wonder Woman'

'She stands for love and compassion
and acceptance and truth, and I think
that those values are so important …
I do believe that if each and every
one of us had a little bit of Wonder
Woman's values, the world would be
a better place.'

Gal Gadot, actress in the title role of
DC's Wonder Woman

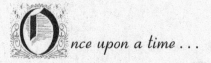

# Once upon a time . . .

. . . a warrior joined the fight for peace.

Diana of Themyscira was an Amazonian princess who grew up surrounded by a legion of warrior women. She loved the ancestral tales of how they bravely defeated evil and brought peace to the world. Queen Hippolyta grew concerned at her daughter's interest in these stories, forbidding her from training to be an Amazon warrior. She wanted to protect her, but she could not stand in the way of Diana's determination.

Armed with the powers of the gods, Diana became the most gifted and courageous fighter of all the Amazons, but also the most compassionate. Her physical strength was matched by the strength of her heart and her faith in peace.

When the world of mankind was threatened by the Olympian God of War, Ares, Diana decided to leave Themyscira so that she could help mankind defeat him, even though it was not her battle to fight. But Diana believed that to know of this evil, and to do nothing, was an evil in itself.

The men and women who fought alongside her named her Wonder Woman.

The true bravery of Diana did not lie in her indestructible bracelets, magical sword, shield or lasso of truth. It was there in the choice that she made to leave behind her home, so that she could take her place in the fight against suffering.

# Elsa

'When you sit back and you just do

what you love, things happen.'

*Idina Menzel, voice of Disney's Elsa*

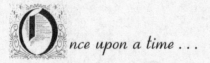

*nce upon a time . . .*

... Queen Elsa of the kingdom of Arendelle stopped pretending.

Having the courage to be yourself can be a daunting prospect, but even more so when the truth might hurt or affect the people you love. Elsa knew this all too well.

Believing herself to be cursed, she struggled in isolation to hide her unique abilities. She was frightened of accidentally hurting someone, especially her younger sister Anna, and was frustrated at the burden of being different. Even when she became queen, she remained self-conscious and reserved, withdrawing from the world around her and doing everything she could to hide who she was.

One day, everything changed, and Elsa could not pretend any longer.

Having spent her life being controlled by fear, Elsa felt a sense of freedom. Finally, she could be true to herself and the unique gifts she had been given, even if that meant being on her own. She embraced her abilities, becoming more daring and confident, taking risks and pushing boundaries to see just how powerful she could be.

Elsa soon realised that running away from the fears of her past could be more damaging than finding the courage to face them. But, whatever storm or blizzard came her way, Elsa was no longer frightened of being herself.

And that was her most magical power of all.

# Modern princesses ...

*work hard*

# Elizabeth II

'I cannot lead you into battle. I do
not give you laws or administer
justice but I can do something
else – I can give my heart and my
devotion to these old islands
and to all the peoples of our
brotherhood of nations.'

*Queen Elizabeth II*

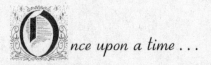

# *O*nce upon a time ...

... a determined princess wanted to serve her country.

During troubled times of war, there are many people who would be relieved to have a title that excused them from working within the armed forces, so that they may carry out their royal duties. Princess Elizabeth was not one of those people.

She went on and on at her father, King George VI, to let her join the forces during the Second World War, even though, as the future queen, it was not expected of her. At first, he tried to change her mind but, in his heart, he knew it was no use fighting the resolve and steadfastness of his 'Lilibet'. He eventually relented.

Signing up to the Auxiliary Territorial Service, the princess became a truck mechanic, deconstructing and rebuilding engines, as well as driving ambulances and military trucks. Dirt got under her nails, grease stained her hands and coveralls; she worked so hard and diligently, she was promoted to Junior Commander within five months. She was the first female member of the British royal family to join the Armed Services.

'I declare before you all,' the princess once said, 'that my whole life, whether it be long or short, shall be devoted to your service.' Four years after this powerful declaration, during a trip to Kenya, she would be told her father had passed away in the night and she was Queen of England.

True to her word, she devoted her life to serving her country, undertaking hundreds of commitments around the world each year and becoming the longest-reigning, hardest-working British monarch.

Just like that stubborn teenager all those years ago, demanding that her father let her do her bit, Elizabeth never hesitated when it came to doing her duty.

# *Fiona*

'Fiona has always been a warrior …

What she has worked for, what

she has fought for, is the love that

she has for herself, for Shrek, for

her family and friends. She has

always been a warrior.'

*Cameron Diaz, voice of*
*Dreamworks Animation's Princess Fiona*

# Once upon a time . . .

. . . an enchanted princess broke the rules.

Princesses are beautiful, fragile and generally waiting around to be rescued by a strong, mighty prince, right? Wrong.

At first, Princess Fiona of Far Far Away did her best to play by the rules. She sat in her tower, guarded by a dragon, and awaited true love's kiss from her Prince Charming.

But when things went awry, Princess Fiona decided that the rules were overrated. This was no damsel in distress. She wasn't going to wait around for a happy ending to come her way; she was going to go ahead and get one for herself.

It's not like she needed a prince to fight her battles for her anyway. What do you think she was doing for all those years locked away in that tower? Singing and daydreaming about a prince? No, she was actually pretty busy becoming an expert in hand-to-hand combat and martial arts.

Like all princesses, Fiona had her fears and challenges – and she had a big secret that she bottled up inside. But she found the courage to hold her head up high and carry on. She realised that she couldn't sit around, hoping that someone else might change things for her. She could make the change herself.

Sometimes, a princess needs to make her own rules.

# Haya

'Remember that, above all else, we are all born free and that no one can put you in a cage except yourself.'

*Princess Haya*

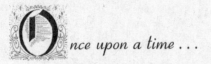 *nce upon a time . . .*

. . . the daughter of a king took the reins.

The young Princess Haya was always getting into trouble, causing plenty of mischief with her brother and feeling like she was always being grounded. Her father, the King of Jordan, would chuckle to himself at this playful streak of hers, but decided that perhaps she needed to learn the importance of discipline, too, and so he introduced her to horses.

It was a whole new world for Princess Haya. At her father's insistence, she had to take care of the horses in her stable: mucking out, brushing the horses down, polishing the tack and managing the training bills. She loved every minute. Her eyes would widen in admiration as she watched show jumping and horse racing on television, before she would dart eagerly to the stables and build her own jumps to practice.

Some people looked down on Princess Haya's passion for riding. 'It is not what princesses do,' voices whispered huffily. But Princess Haya was galloping much too fast to hear those voices. She trained so hard that she competed in national competitions and then in international events.

She became the first woman to represent Jordan in international equestrian sport and the only woman to win a medal in the Pan-Arab Equestrian Games.

This trailblazing princess didn't just lead the way in sport. She took on humanitarian roles, tackling hunger, poverty and illiteracy.

No matter how big the hurdle, Princess Haya wouldn't back down. She would simply have to jump even higher.

# Tiana

'She's a huge dreamer. But she's also the type of person who, after dreaming that dream, then goes to sit down to make a plan to attain it.'

*Anika Noni Rose, voice of Disney's Princess Tiana*

*O*nce upon a time . . .

. . . an ambitious young woman didn't let anything stop her.

Growing up in New Orleans, Tiana was a talented chef from a young age, encouraged by her hard-working parents. Her father beamed proudly as she told him about her dream to one day open the grandest restaurant around, with sparkling chandeliers, jazz bands and the most delicious food you ever tasted.

He had no doubt that she would achieve her dream one day. He often reminded her that if she worked hard, she could achieve anything she set her mind to.

And so the determined Tiana got to work. She knew that there were others who had it easier in life, but that did not intimidate her. With patience and a strong will, she would get there her own way.

Tiana's resourcefulness and intelligence intrigued and inspired the free-spirited Prince Naveen of Maldonia, who had grown up in privilege, lacking any kind of responsibility or ambition.

There were times when Tiana had moments of doubt, when her hopes began to slip away and all the hard work appeared to amount to nothing. But she journeyed on, holding to the faith that if you put your mind to a dream, whatever that dream may be, nothing and no one can stand in your way.

Modern
princesses
... are
*smart*

# Lalla Salma

'When hope is combined with

hard work and generosity, life

is given a second chance.'

*Princess Lalla Salma*

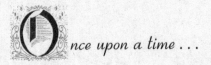

# Once upon a time ...

... a king was dazzled by a young woman's knowledge.

King Mohammed VI of Morocco was at a party when he stepped into the path of a woman with fiery red hair. It was the beginning of a powerful love story; one that would change the history of their country.

Salma Bennani stood out at school, not just for her striking red hair, but for her keen mind. Salma loved learning. Fascinated by different cultures and countries, Salma studied four languages: Arabic, French, English and Spanish. She was also intrigued by science – how knowledge and communication could be powerful tools for social change. She became valedictorian at a top engineering school in Morocco, earned a degree in computer science and got a job as a computer engineer.

When King Mohammed VI met the bright, hard-working Salma, he knew she was the woman he wanted to marry. His devotion to Salma sparked many firsts for the nation: she became the first commoner to marry into royalty; she was the first wife of a Moroccan king to be granted a royal title; and, up until their union, it had been tradition for the king not to reveal the name of his bride in public, but King Mohammed VI officially announced his marriage to her in the media.

Salma Bennani shone much too brightly to be hidden away in the shadows.

Her commitment to scientific research led her to set up the Lalla Salma Foundation for the prevention and treatment of cancer. The organisation improved training and care, and has funded research institutions around the world.

Through the power of knowledge, Princess Lalla Salma turned hope into reality.

# Leia

'She was our great and powerful

princess – feisty, wise and

full of hope.'

*George Lucas, creator and director of Star Wars*

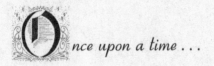

# Once upon a time . . .

... a fearless princess led a resistance.

In a distant galaxy, Princess Leia Organa of Alderaan dedicated her life to fighting against tyranny and oppression.

Acknowledging the dangers and sacrifices that would come with such a mission against the dark, powerful force known as The Empire, Leia did not hesitate to lead her people towards the battlefield.

A cunning diplomat and brave warrior, Princess Leia commanded respect by not only taking charge, but also by taking her place in the fighting line. She spoke her mind and was unwilling to compromise on her principles. This princess was capable of rescuing herself, often shooting out witty remarks at the same time as shooting a blaster pistol.

Leia turned her grief from personal losses into resilience and strength: the more evil she came up against, the more determined she became to beat it, no matter what the cost.

Whether in battle or her beliefs, Princess Leia refused to surrender. She was, and always will be, a never-faltering beacon of hope, shining bright amongst the stars.

# Kiko

'It will be like a new wind blowing

in the imperial household.'

*Prime Minister Toshiki Kaifu, on Princess Kiko*

# Once upon a time . . .

. . . a princess spoke without saying a word.

Kiko Kawashima was studying psychology when one evening she took a break to attend the theatre. There, she saw a play performed entirely in Japanese Sign Language. Kiko was utterly mesmerised by the extraordinary skill and beauty of this form of communication. She glanced around at those in the audience with hearing impairments, and saw they were enraptured and entertained by the storytelling.

Imagine, she thought, if sign language did not exist. Everyone deserves the right to storytelling; the right to express their feelings and opinions; the right to have access to the feelings and opinions of others. She was going to learn this wonderful new language.

When Prince Akishino met Kiko at university, he fell head over heels for this intelligent, compassionate young woman.

While Princess Kiko continued her education, gaining an MA in psychology and a PhD, she was also on a mission to break barriers. She spoke at conferences and high-school speech contests, passionately calling for a better understanding of those with hearing impairments. She visited schools for deaf children, attended plays performed in sign language and became an active supporter of the Deaflympics. She encouraged her children to learn Japanese Sign Language, so that they too could help raise awareness.

On a visit to a deaf centre in America, a photographer captured a moment when the princess was signing with a student there. Smiling broadly, Princess Kiko raised her hand, using American Sign Language to communicate a sentiment for which there are no barriers, not even those of language: 'I love you.'

# Maha Chakri Sirindhorn

'Access to education is a fundamental human right. Education provides opportunity to learn and live sufficiently.'

*Princess Maha Chakri Sirindhorn*

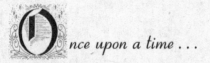

# Once upon a time ...

... a princess could not stop asking questions.

It didn't matter who she was with, where she was or what she was talking about, Princess Maha was fascinated by the subject at hand. She was so curious, that she carried a notebook wherever she went to make sure she could jot down all the lovely new information she learnt every day.

At school, she loved to hear about the history of her kingdom, Thailand. She achieved a first-class degree and a gold medal in the arts, writing beautiful poetry and stories, and painting. She continued her studies and received MA degrees in Oriental Epigraphy and Pali-Sanskrit, then a doctoral degree in development education. Along the way, she learned English, French, Mandarin Chinese, German and Latin.

The compassionate, intelligent princess believed the more she could learn, the more she could help her country. *Click! Click!* people heard as their beloved princess came to visit, taking pictures with the camera hanging round her neck, and writing notes into her book.

Once, she visited a remote rural village where children were suffering from malnutrition. She studied her notes and photos, and asked plenty of questions, until she thought of a long-term solution. She could set up an agriculture project, for which the children plant vegetables and raise laying hens at their school. They could turn the produce into their lunch *and* learn useful farming skills. It worked so well, her initiative was introduced into more than 700 schools. And that was only one of her hundreds of brilliant ideas.

Her nation gave her the affectionate name of *Phra Thep*, meaning 'Princess Angel'. That is what she was in their eyes: an angel walking among them, busy scribbling away in her notebook.

Modern princesses
...are
kind

# Diana

'Only do what your heart tells you.'

*Princess Diana*

# Once upon a time . . .

. . . a princess held a sick man's hand and changed the world.

Diana had arrived at a London hospital to open the UK's first unit dedicated to treating patients with HIV and AIDS. Although things are different now, at the time, people were terrified of this disease and shunned those suffering from it, scared that it would spread.

Diana didn't see it that way. When she sat down opposite an AIDS patient that day at the hospital, she only saw someone who was very ill and who needed compassion and love.

She reached out and took his hand in hers.

Diana challenged the irrational fear that the disease could be spread by touch and she reminded us that everyone deserves to be loved, not by saying that, but by showing it.

From the moment she married Prince Charles, she worked hard to shed light on important issues. She walked across an active minefield in Angola to bring attention to those who had been affected by landmines; she visited homeless centres, listening to the stories of those seeking refuge there; she went to hospitals and sat with the sick.

'They all need to be loved while they are here,' she said. 'I try to be there for them.'

Princess Diana's belief that simple acts can change the world lives on in the millions of people showing kindness to those who feel unloved and forgotten.

# Catherine

'Imagine if everyone was able to help just one child who needs to be listened to, needs to be respected, and needs to be loved – we could make such a huge difference for an entire generation.'

*Duchess of Cambridge*

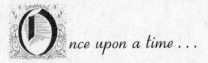

# Once upon a time . . .

. . . Catherine decided it was about time we talked.

Since marrying the man she'd fallen in love with at university, Prince William, the future King of England, the Duchess of Cambridge had thrown herself into royal duties, meeting vulnerable young people, working with homeless shelters and supporting charities that helped those with illnesses. Despite the variety of all her philanthropic work, Catherine couldn't help but notice an unspoken similarity at the heart of many of the problems people faced: mental health.

'We can't talk about that,' some would say.

Catherine wanted to talk about it. Because if nobody talked about mental health issues, then somebody suffering with them might think they were different. They might feel ashamed by it. They might be too afraid of judgement to admit they're struggling. They might think they were all alone. Catherine didn't want them to feel alone any longer.

'Sometimes,' she said firmly, 'it's just a simple conversation that can make things better.'

Catherine voiced an idea to her husband and her brother-in-law, Prince Harry, and, with their help, she launched a campaign called Heads Together. It tackled the stigma surrounding mental health, encouraged people to talk, and reached out to those afraid to ask for help. Something miraculous started to happen.

'I struggle with mental health,' people said, inspired by the campaign. 'Me too,' others would reply. And then they didn't feel so alone.

Catherine continued to spark conversation across the land. Because with each voice, came more hope.

# Grace

'I would like to be remembered

as trying to do my job well, being

understanding and kind … I'd like

to be remembered as a decent

human being and a caring one.'

*Princess Grace*

# O nce upon a time . . .

. . . a girl named Grace loved to dance.

Shy and reserved growing up, Grace Kelly found somewhere tranquil to escape to, a place she felt most at home: the dance studio. She dreamed of stepping into a spotlight and dazzling an audience.

Growing up to become a famous Hollywood actress, Grace seemed to glide across the screen with her beautiful poise and elegance. While her beauty and talent entranced audiences, her warm and generous spirit captured the heart of Prince Rainier of Monaco.

Stepping into her busy royal role, she set about achieving her new dream: to bring the magic of performing arts to children, so that they too might have the chance to stand centre stage. She established the Princess Grace Foundation, supporting young artists; set up the Princess Grace Dance Academy; and initiated the International Monte-Carlo Ballet Festival, gathering together the world's dancers to perform and inspire.

When she died, her family knew it was important to honour her sparkling passion for helping young artists achieve their dreams. They launched the Princess Grace Foundation in the USA, to award scholarships and fellowships, and established a ballet company in Monaco, Les Ballets de Monte-Carlo, something Princess Grace had always hoped to do.

# Máxima

'People in the street call me Máxima.
At the end of the day, it's not that
important to be called princess or
queen. The important thing is
the title we represent.'

*Queen Máxima*

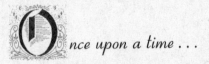

*nce upon a time ...*

... Máxima thought the world should be more colourful.

With a personality as bright and cheerful as the clothes that she wore, she caught the eye of a young man named 'Alexander', who happened to be the heir to the Dutch throne – not that he admitted that teeny, tiny detail to her when they first met. In fact, when he finally did slip it into conversation that he was the prince and future king of the Netherlands, Máxima's first reaction was to laugh ... until she realised he was being perfectly serious.

Prince Willem-Alexander proposed and the people of the Netherlands came to adore their new princess: down-to-earth, kind, funny, unconventional and always bringing a splash of colour wherever she went.

But, for Máxima, the world wasn't as colourful as she would have hoped; long shadows of discrimination clashed with the bright rainbow colours of the lesbian, gay, bisexual and trans community. There was still plenty of work and campaigning to do to ensure freedom and equal rights for all.

Up until then, no member of the royal family had ever taken a public stance on this important issue. But, as in everything else, Princess Máxima wasn't a fan of following the crowd.

She decided to show her full support for LGBT rights and equality by attending an LGBT conference, drawing media attention from all over the world. She visited schools, discussing sexual diversity with students, and, when her husband ascended the throne, one of her first appearances as queen was at a two-day international gay-rights summit in The Hague.

Queen Máxima wanted the world to know that everyone had the right to show their true colours, whatever they may be.

# Rania

'I always find that, with women, if you empower them a little bit, they lift everyone around them. Education for girls is the best investment you can make, because the ripple effect affects so many issues – health, child mortality, economic empowerment all benefit when you give girls an education.'

Queen Rania

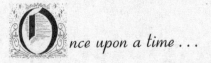

# Once upon a time . . .

. . . Queen Rania of Jordan sat down and wrote a story.

Sometimes, you are hit so hard and fast by a jolt of inspiration that you have to sit down right away and scribble down the story so that it can never be forgotten. That is exactly what happened to Queen Rania. She had met a young woman, who told her about many great obstacles she had had to overcome to earn an education, and Queen Rania knew instantly it was a story that needed to be told.

Children sigh all over the world at the idea of going to school. But Queen Rania wanted to show children that education was the most powerful tool of all. It brought tolerance and love; inspired confidence and respect. It transformed and empowered communities and, in turn, the world. To be able to learn was a gift. And Queen Rania wanted more than anything to make it an unquestionable human right.

So, she sat down at her desk and wrote a story about Maha of the Mountains, a courageous girl determined to go to school even though she has to walk miles down a desert road and face anger from people in her village, who do not believe girls should be educated. But Maha doesn't give up.

Children in classrooms read the queen's story.

Queen Rania renovated more than 500 schools in Jordan, launched scholarship programmes and literacy initiatives. She travelled all over the world advocating for the right of every child on the planet to go to school, so that someday they might have all the tools they need to tell their own story.

Modern
princesses
... are
*ahead of their time*

# Margaret

'She was a multifaceted and
brilliant person with an underlying
simplicity and strength.'

*Lord St John of Fawsley, on Princess Margaret*

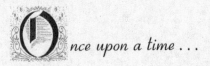

*nce upon a time . . .*

... a princess stood apart from the crowd.

Vibrant, eccentric and fond of a little mischief every now and then, the younger sister of Queen Elizabeth II lived in a time when, as the princess, she was expected to say certain things, meet certain people and act a certain way. But Princess Margaret was too full of life to let anyone confine her to a cage.

Her father, King George VI, loved and indulged her vivacious nature. 'Elizabeth is my pride,' he would say of his eldest, the future queen, and then he would get a twinkle in his eye, 'and Margaret is my joy.' The princess loved music and dancing. She was so intelligent and witty, read countless books and would always have her friends in stitches. She listened to jazz and became friends with actors, photographers and musicians, fascinated by their flair and freedom.

Rebelling against expectations is never an easy path. Whispers began on corners and then they spread on to streets, seeping through into the palace. 'She's too wild and reckless to be a princess,' they said.

Margaret heard the voices, but she did not bow to them. She smiled in the face of their frowns. She was daring and defiant. She made her own rules, loyal to her belief that no woman should have their destiny chosen for them.

And if you look closely at her pictures, you can see it there in her eyes, the spirited spark that the world would come to admire after her death.

'Life is to be lived,' it seems to say. 'No one can tell you who you should be.'

# Elizabeth I

'I have the heart and stomach of a

king, and a king of England too.'

Queen Elizabeth I

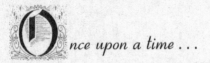 *nce upon a time . . .*

. . . a princess believed in herself.

When her mother was sentenced to death by her father, the notorious King Henry VIII, Princess Elizabeth was in turn doomed to a neglected childhood, sent away from her father to live under the care of governesses and later imprisoned in the Tower of London by her half-sister, Queen Mary. Steely and astute, the princess dedicated her time to her studies, becoming a great scholar in languages and politics and, importantly, the art of public speaking. Princess Elizabeth recognised the power of rhetoric.

From the very beginning of her reign, when she ascended the throne at the age of twenty-five, Queen Elizabeth was pressured to marry. That was what female monarchs did, her advisors told her.

'Women have weak hearts and a weak will,' they stated.

Elizabeth did not feel weak. She felt as strong as the lions on the English royal coat of arms that waved on her flags. She broke the rules and refused to marry.

'I am already bound unto a husband,' she retorted to those who doubted her, 'which is the kingdom of England.'

She knew that she could rule her country as shrewdly and with as much strength and devotion as any man.

On the day her troops faced an invasion, she went to offer them a rallying speech.

'I myself will take up arms,' she declared as they stood in awe. 'I myself will be your general.' Her words were so powerful that they would be remembered for centuries.

Queen Elizabeth I is renowned as a great leader. She was ahead of her time in recognising the importance of connecting with her people.

Her advisors had been wrong all along. She did not need to seek strength in marriage; she sought it within herself.

# Pingyang

'She was no ordinary woman.'

*Li Yuan, Emperor Gaozu of Tang, on his daughter,*
*Princess Pingyang*

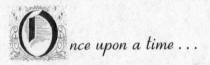
*nce upon a time . . .*

The Emperor Yangdi, who was renowned for his brutality and his desire for power, ruled China. His people suffered under his evil rule and they yearned for a revolt. When they began to look to Pingyang's father, Li Yuan, a brave military commander, to save them, the Emperor was furious. Li Yuan went into hiding, secretly raising rebel forces.

Only twenty years old and a woman, Pingyang was expected to stay in hiding too, so that she would not be imprisoned. But she could not hide away and do nothing while people suffered and her father was in danger. She came up with a plan.

Knowing that many were starving due to a devastating drought, Pingyang opened the food stores on her estate, saving many lives. Then she called on the people to join her in a rebellion. They did not hesitate, proudly naming themselves the 'Woman's Army'.

She reached out to other rebel groups, using her resourcefulness and skills of negotiation to bring them together as one united force under her leadership. They pledged their service to this extraordinarily fearless female general.

Pingyang led the Woman's Army to victory after victory against Yangdi's forces, ensuring that after each battle, food was distributed to the grateful civilians in each liberated territory. More troops eagerly joined her ranks and, alongside her father's and brother's army, Pingyang defeated Yangdi once and for all.

It was the beginning of what would be known as the prosperous Golden Age in Chinese history. Dying just a few years after the revolt, Princess Pingyang was hailed as a true heroine, whose courage brought hope to a nation and whose memory would never fade.

# Hatshepsut

'I have restored that which

was in ruins.'

*Queen Hatshepsut*

*O*nce upon a time . . .

... a forgotten woman built a kingdom.

When Hatshepsut ascended the Egyptian throne after her husband's death, many questioned whether a woman should be pharaoh. But Hatshepsut stood her ground, trusting her ability to not only rule Egypt, but make it all the greater.

Turning her back on violence and military gain, her long reign was one of peace, as she instead devoted resources to expanding the country's trade networks, increasing Egypt's wealth. With her encouragement, sculpture and decorative arts flourished, but it was for her building ambitions that she came to be known.

She constructed statues and grand obelisks at Karnak, restored monuments that had been destroyed, and commissioned the building of the famous Temple of Pakhet, an underground shrine dedicated to the lioness goddess. Her tomb, the breathtaking Mortuary Temple of Hatshepsut, is considered her greatest achievement and an architectural masterpiece.

Doubts over Hatshepsut's abilities faded away and statues were built in her honour; some, on her orders, depicted her as a male king, with the traditional beard and royal regalia of a pharaoh.

However, great success can breed fear and jealousy. After her death, her successors grew afraid that the memory of a triumphant female pharaoh would damage the traditional notion of male rule. They set about eliminating all memory of her, tearing down and smashing her statues, chiselling her image off stone walls, and erasing her name from written records. As the days turned to years, turned to decades, turned to centuries, Hatshepsut was forgotten.

But all was not lost. Egyptologists began to piece together this great forgotten ruler and gradually her achievements came to light. Hatshepsut has finally been given her rightful place in history as one of the most successful pharaohs of Egypt.

For nothing, not even the might of kings, can bury the truth.

# Nzinga

'One of the greatest of the
African warrior queens.'

*Historian John Henrik Clarke,
on Queen Nzinga*

# Once upon a time . . .

. . . Nzinga would not bow to bullies.

A long time ago, when Angola was known as the kingdom of Ndongo, a princess witnessed Portuguese ships land on the shores of south-west Africa. The people on these ships mercilessly took prisoners for the growing slave trade and plotted to conquer Ndongo.

Princess Nzinga's brother, the king, sent her to negotiate with these invaders in the hope that she might be able to convince them to leave Ndongo. Unafraid, and with her head held high, Nzinga went to the meeting and refused to be bullied by these powerful men. She commanded their respect with her diplomatic ability and intelligence. They agreed to her terms of peace and Nzinga returned home.

But, the men did not stay true to their word for long, pushing their forces into Ndongo and betraying their promise to Nzinga. Her people were forced from their homes, fleeing to the kingdom of

Matamba. By then, the king had passed away and Nzinga was queen, shouldering the responsibility of fighting for her homeland.

'She will soon give up,' the invaders sneered, as Nzinga called on her people to take up arms and help her reclaim their land and their freedom. 'She cannot fight us forever.'

They were wrong. Such was her passion, Nzinga would never stop fighting for her country. She knew that to defeat her enemy, she would need a bigger army, so she forged alliances with others and provided sanctuary for runaway slaves, earning their loyalty and service. She gained notoriety for personally leading her troops into war.

Having battled the Portuguese for decades, Nzinga passed away peacefully in her eighties, leaving a lasting legacy: the fight against oppression is nothing to do with where you stand on the ground; it is where you stand in your heart.

# Seondeok

'Queen Seondeok was a great

woman in history.'

*Lee Yo Won, actress in the
title role of the 2009 film Queen Seondeok*

# Once upon a time . . .

. . . a princess looked to the stars.

Many years ago, when Korea was split into three, the ruler of the kingdom of Silla did not have a son, but three daughters. As King Jinpyeong got old, the idea of having a female ruler worried the people of Silla, especially in a time of upheaval among the three nations – their future was uncertain. But the king had noticed one of his daughters, the heir to the throne, gazing up at the stars, her eyes filled with wonder and curiosity. He knew that his kingdom was in safe hands.

On ascending the throne, the intelligent and cautious Queen Seondeok was the first female ruler of the kingdom, and she knew from the start that her reign would be steeped in conflict. She would face attacks not only from Silla's enemies hoping to conquer the land, but also from those within her kingdom who could not abide the idea of a woman at their helm. They had no faith in their new queen. Seondeok could not afford to waste any time.

She formed a significant alliance with China, strengthening Silla's power against its rivals.

Intellectually superior and devoted to the arts, the queen encouraged a renaissance in thought and the exchange of ideas, as well as literature and the arts. She promoted peace between different religious groups, and her fascination with the stars never faded. She went on to build the Cheomseongdae, a star-gazing tower and the first astronomical observatory in east Asia.

'What good is that?' some wondered, shaking their heads. But from star-gazing, they learned to forecast the weather, improving farming and relieving poverty.

'There is so much wonder in the world,' Queen Seondeok thought, smiling to herself, 'if we only take the time to look up at the stars and notice it.'

*The End*

*Thank You*

# Acknowledgements

Huge thanks to Laura and the fantastic team at Ebury for giving me the opportunity to write this book. I have loved every moment of its creation and feel very lucky to have worked with you.

Special thanks to my agent, Lauren, one of the most inspirational and genius women I know, and to everyone at the Bell Lomax Moreton Agency.

Big thanks to the ridiculously talented Angeline Balayn for bringing these words to life with such beautiful illustrations.

As always, my friends and family must be thanked and congratulated for putting up with me during the writing process.

To all you princesses out there, this book is for you. Thank you for continuing to inspire, sacrifice and work hard to bring about change for the better. Thank you for speaking out for unheard voices and for leading the charge, even when it's not easy. Thank you for reminding us all of the strength within ourselves.

It's true, you know. Whether you have a crown or not, if you believe you're a princess, then you are a princess.

And long may you reign.

# Quotation
# Sources

Page 5
*A Little Princess* by Francis Hodgson Burnett,
first published in 1905

Page 13
'With Fame Comes Opportunity but Also a
Responsibility', written by Meghan Markle for
*ELLE* in November 2016

Page 17
*Auli'i Cravalho on Voicing Moana and Feeling Like
Beyoncé Harpers Bazaar* November 2016

Page 21
Every effort has been made to find the original
source for this quote, but we first read it in
the article 'Here Are 10 of Princess Ameerah
Al-Taweel's Most Inspirational Quotes'
*Emirates Woman*, November 2017

Page 25
'Gal Gadot Felt 'Privileged' To Play
Wonder Woman: 'I Adore This Character'',
*Entertainment Weekly*, May 2016

Page 29
'Idina Menzel's Fairy Tale Journey:
From Broadway to 'Frozen' and a 'Gorgeous'
Note From John Travolta', *Billboard*,
March 2014

Page 35
(www.royal.uk) The 1957 Christmas
Broadcast

Page 39
The press conference given by the cast of
*Shrek* in Hollywood, May 2010

Page 43
"I Am Far From Perfect': Princess Haya
Opens Up In Rare Interview', *Emirates Woman*,
October 2016

Page 47
Taken from the video 'Anika Noni Rose in
The Princess and the Frog' on Youtube channel
'BlacktreeTV' in 2009

Page 53
Taken from a speech given by Princess Lalla
Salma at the charity gala for the construction
of an Oncology Center in Beni Mellal,
Morocco on 3rd October 2015

Page 57
'Our Great and Powerful Princess: George
Lucas Remembers Carrie Fisher', *Time*,
December 2016

Page 61
'Scenes From an Uncommon Marriage:
Japan's Prince Aya Weds a Cinderella Psych
Major, Kiko Kawashima', *People.com,* July 2016

Page 65
Taken from Princess Maha Chakri Sirindhorn's
speech delivered in the Food and Nutrition
Seminar at Mahidol University, Salaya,
Thailand, on 17th August 2005

Page 71
Every effort has been made to find the original
source of this quote.

Page 75
Taken from a speech given by the Duchess
of Cambridge at the Pace2Be Headteacher
Conference, London, UK, on 18th November
2015

Page 79
Taken from an interview given by Princess Grace on ABC's *20/20* with Pierre Salinger, 22nd June 1982

Page 83
Taken from an interview given by TRH the Prince of Orange and Princess Máxima on RTL news, 17th April 2013

Page 87
'The Interview: Queen Rania of Jordan on the Refugee Crisis, Isis and Being a Muslim Woman', *The Times*, April 2017

Page 93
'Prince Tells of His Deep Sadness', *The Telegraph*, February 2002

Page 97
Taken from the Speech to the Troops at
Tilbury given by Queen Elizabeth I in 1558,
found on a manuscript at the British Library

Page 101
Taken from an historical quote attributed to
Li Yuan, Emperor Gaozu of Tang

Page 105
Taken from an historical quote attributed to
Queen Hatshepsut

Page 109
Every effort has been made to find the original
source of this quote.

Page 113
Taken from the article 'Feisty Bossy Roll Gets
the Thumbs Up From Actress', *Straitstimes.com,*
August 2016

2

Pop Press, an imprint of Ebury Publishing,
20 Vauxhall Bridge Road,
London, SW1V 2SA

Pop Press is part of the Penguin Random House group of companies
whose addresses can be found at global.penguinrandomhouse.com

First published by Ebury Press in 2018
This paperback edition published in 2022

www.penguin.co.uk

A CIP catalogue record for this book is available from the British Library

Design: Seagull Design

ISBN: 9781529909692

Typeset in 11/17 Garamond MT Std
by Integra Software Services Pvt Ltd, Pondicherry

Printed and bound in Great Britain by Clays Ltd, St Ives PLC

Penguin Random House is committed to a sustainable future
for our business, our readers and our planet. This book is
made from Forest Stewardship Council® certified paper.